Magic Kingdom® Park

Main Street, U.S.A.®

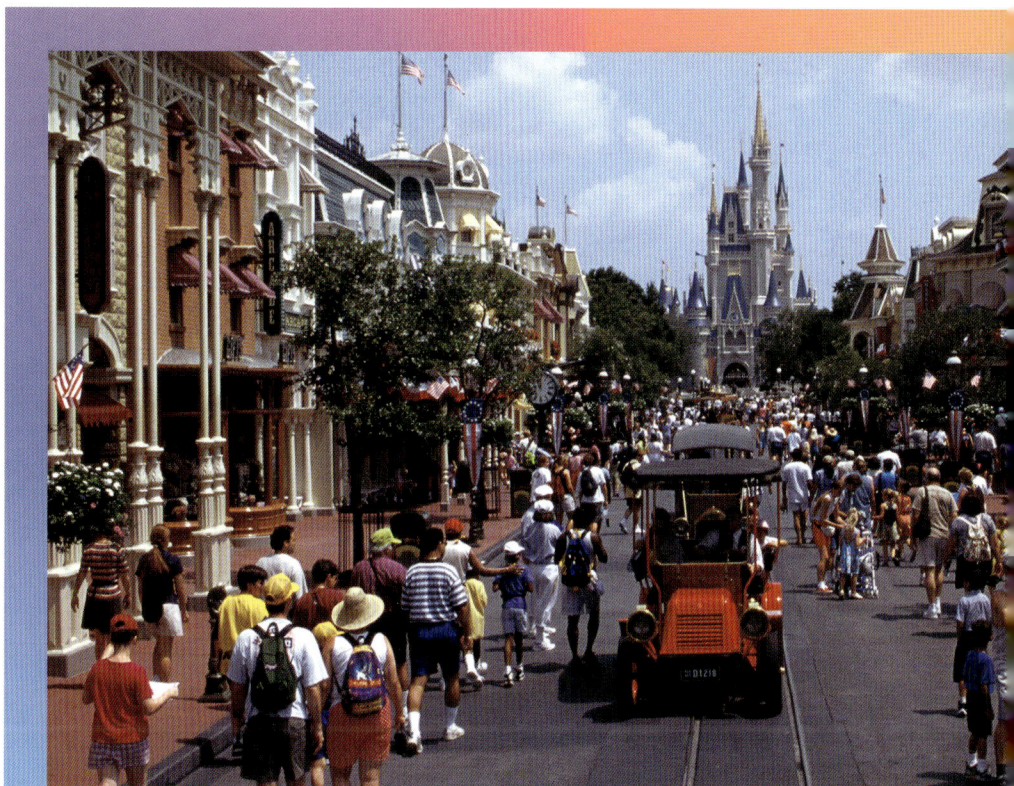

The picture-perfect sights and sounds of turn-of-the-century America welcome guests to Magic Kingdom Park on Main Street, U.S.A. The colorful thoroughfare is an idealized version of what small-town America was like when Walter Elias Disney was a young boy. Horse-drawn streetcars and honking jitneys carry guests past gingerbread Victorian storefronts as the magnificent fairy tale castle beckons from the end of the street.

Elegant charm and an attention to detail help evoke the nostalgia of small-town America on Main Street, U.S.A., with such places as the Main Street Confectionery, above, which stocks hundreds of sweet treats, or an old-time barbershop, opposite top right, where a child can delight in his first haircut. "Partners," opposite near left, a bronze statue of Walt Disney and Mickey Mouse, extends an invitation of fun to the entire family. In the Share A Dream Come True™ Parade down Main Street, opposite far left, beloved Disney characters appear inside giant snow globes. The distinctive Crystal Palace, right, is a showstopper at night with its outline of glittering lights.

Adventureland®

Cast off on a jungle cruise, brave a pirate attack . . . your imagination and the magic of Disney take you to lands of tropical splendor—the Caribbean, Polynesia, and Southeast Asia—for countless exciting adventures. Lush landscaping, splashing waterfalls, and a distant drumbeat add to the ambience.

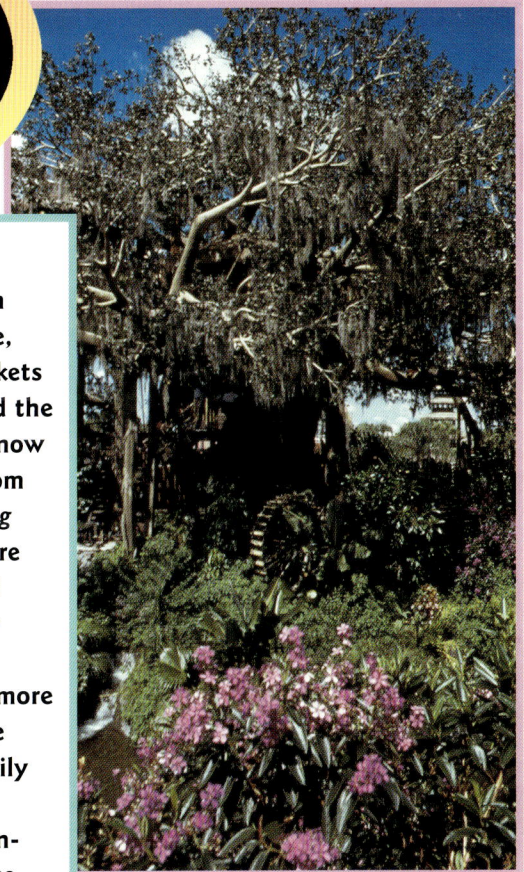

The shops and stalls of Caribbean Plaza's exotic marketplace, opposite, offer strolling explorers unique trinkets and souvenirs imported from around the globe. The Enchanted Tiki Room is now Under New Management as Iago from *Aladdin* and Zazu from *The Lion King* try to supervise its zany cast of more than 225 singing birds, flowers, and tiki statues. Right, the Swiss Family Treehouse looks surprisingly real; 300,000 lifelike leaves sprout from more than 1,000 branches. A climb to the top takes you past bedrooms, a family room, and a kitchen. An ingenious rope-and-pulley system supplies running water throughout the treehouse.

The classic and colorful Pirates of the Caribbean puts you right in the middle of a raid on a Caribbean town by raucous buccaneers. Guests begin their adventure by boat in the darkness of a pirates' den, only to intrude upon the swashbucklers as they wreak havoc to the tune of "Yo Ho, Yo Ho, a Pirate's Life for Me."

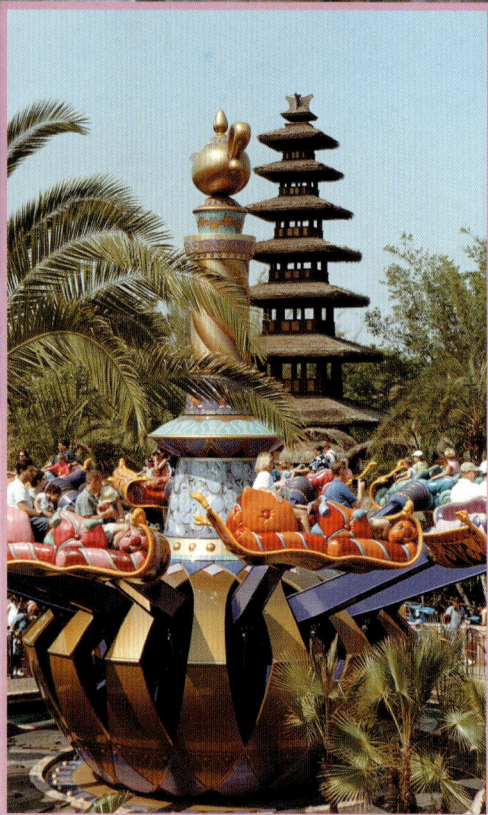

Beside the Agrabah Bazaar, The Magic Carpets of Aladdin whirl guests around a large Genie lamp into a whole new world of fun. Riders can control the side to side and tilting movements of their flying carpet, which may help them avoid the nearby water-spitting camels!

Liberty Square

Colonial America comes to life in Liberty Square. Guests journey back to the days of riverboat travel, quaint clapboard shops, grand Georgian buildings, and long, leisurely strolls down wide cobblestone streets. The Liberty Tree, a majestic live oak, has 13 lanterns hanging from its branches in honor of the 13 original colonies.

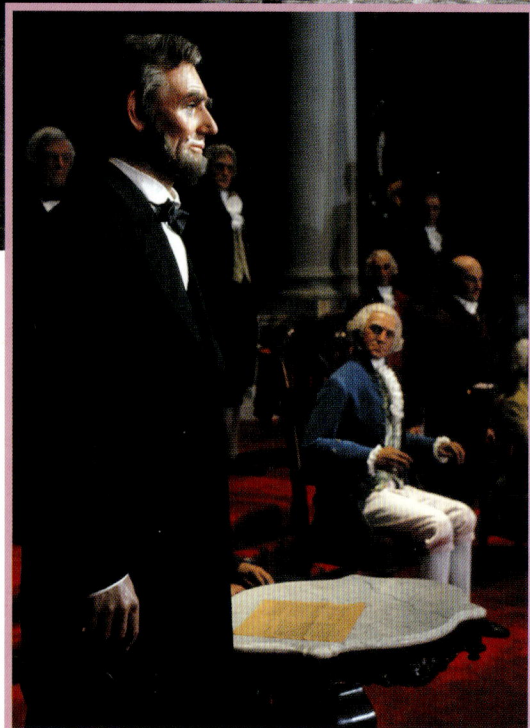

The Haunted Mansion looms behind the *Liberty Belle* riverboat, a real steamboat with a boiler that turns water into steam to drive the paddle wheel that propels the boat through the Rivers of America. At left, Abraham Lincoln makes a stirring speech in the Hall of Presidents, where guests get an entertaining look at the 43 chief executives of the United States. Though all the presidents appear amazingly real, President George W. Bush has the only other speaking role.

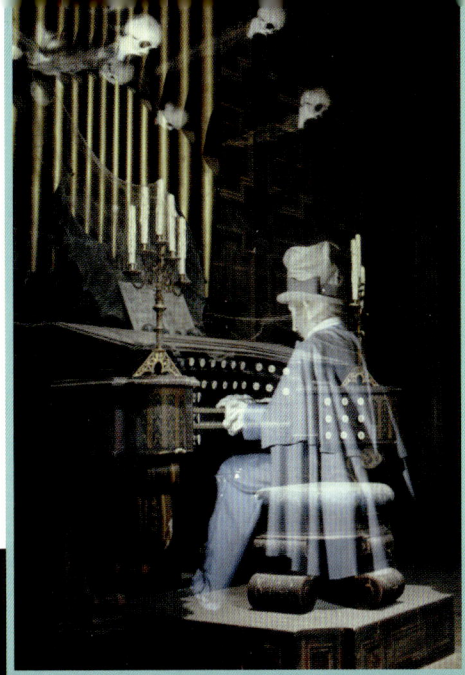

Grinning ghosts greet visitors on a spooky journey through The Haunted Mansion, a dusty old house full of special effects. Voices howl and phantoms dance in the darkness, but it's all just good-spirited fun.

FRONTIERLAND®

The runaway mine cars of Big Thunder Mountain Railroad, left, race to escape the boom—literally—and bust of the Gold Rush–era mining town of Tumbleweed. Below, Harper's Mill welcomes visitors arriving by raft to Tom Sawyer Island, where there are caves to explore and hills to climb—a cool respite in the midst of Magic Kingdom Park.

The American Frontier in all its wild glory is revisited in Frontierland. The red rock of Big Thunder Mountain Railroad creates a believable backdrop for this land, which pays tribute to America's pioneer spirit. Step back to the 1800s, to the days of rugged mining towns and uncharted adventures as Americans moved westward.

A hand-clappin', toe-tappin' good time awaits at the Country Bear Jamboree in Grizzly Hall. Three seasonal shows offer clever and comical performances by a cast of furry creatures, including some wry commentary from the mounted animal heads. Opposite page, riders may not notice the awesome view of the Magic Kingdom from high atop Splash Mountain just before the log flume takes a five-story plunge into the briar patch. Based on the animated Disney film *Song of the South*, the watery trip through swamps and bayous tells the classic story of B'rer Rabbit, B'rer Bear, and B'rer Fox.

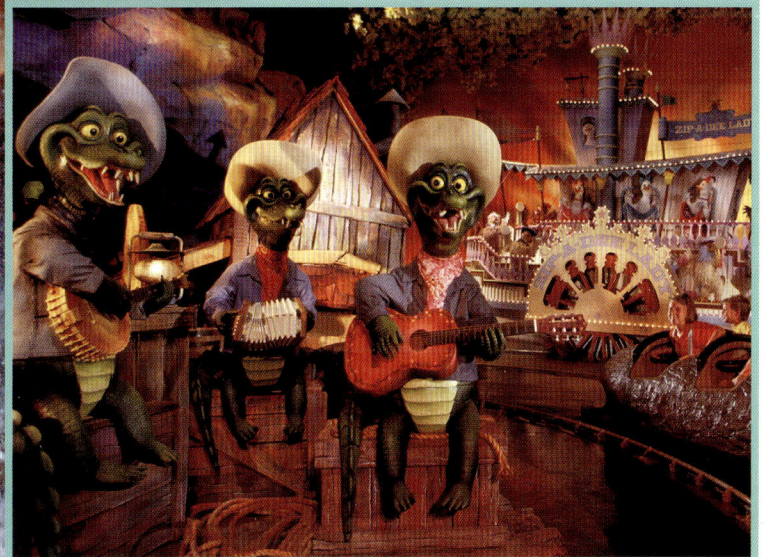

Fantasyland®

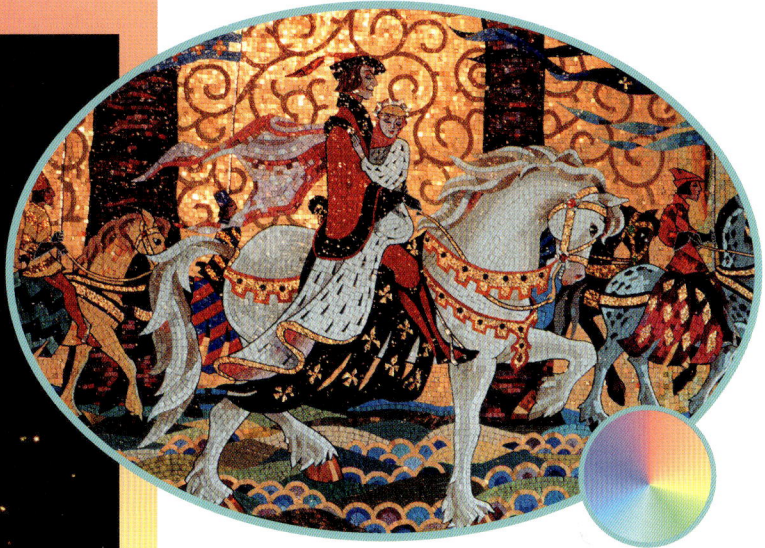

Elaborate murals in Cinderella Castle tell the story of the little cinder girl. These brilliant artworks use a million pieces of Italian glass in about 500 different colors, fused with real silver and 14-karat gold. Even though the castle's architects studied famous European palaces and castles, Cinderella Castle is made of steel and fiberglass, with no real stone.

Fantasyland is where dreams come true, in a place of colorful canopies and gleaming turrets reminiscent of a medieval fair. Step through the spectacular corridor of Cinderella Castle and into the pages of delightful storybooks. Whimsical attractions feature characters from *Peter Pan*, *Snow White*, *Cinderella*, *Dumbo*, and *The Lion King*. It's enchanting for children of all ages.

Disney magic meets Disney music in *Mickey's PhilharMagic*, a new 3-D film spectacular. Accompanied by a dazzling array of in-theater effects, Mickey, Donald, Ariel, Aladdin, Jasmine, and Simba star in an eye-popping experience that unfolds on one of the largest screens ever created for a 3-D film.

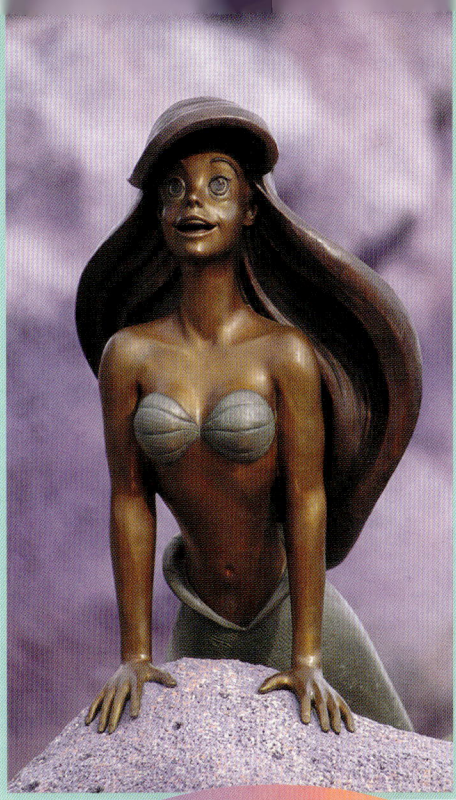

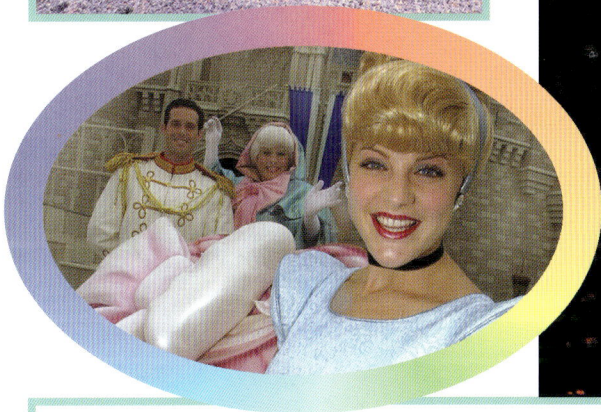

The entrance to Ariel's Grotto, where guests can meet a live "mermaid," is marked by a statue, top, of *The Little Mermaid*. Above, audience members enjoy music and merriment at Cinderella's Surprise Celebration. Cinderella's Golden Carrousel, right, is a favorite among children. Originally built in 1917, it has been completely renovated with scenes from *Cinderella* hand-painted on 18 panels above the horses.

Snow White's Scary Adventures, left, depicts several scenes inspired by *Snow White and the Seven Dwarfs*, the world's first animated feature film, created by Walt Disney in 1937. Guests follow Snow White on a journey through the forest where she encounters the wicked witch. In Peter Pan's Flight, opposite page, guests take off in soaring pirate ships over the rooftops of London. Along the way to Never Land, they meet Tinker Bell, Captain Hook, and Tiger Lily, among other favorites. The droll adventures of everybody's favorite "chubby little cubby" come to life in The Many Adventures of Winnie the Pooh, far right, a magical journey through the Hundred Acre Wood.

Winnie the Pooh Characters Based on the "Winnie-the-Pooh" Works by A.A. Milne and E.H. Shepard

A relaxing boat ride takes guests through the many lands of It's a Small World, an attraction originally created for the 1964–65 New York World's Fair. Hundreds of singing dolls represent more than 100 cultures from around the globe. The unforgettable theme song, sung in different languages as guests pass through the attraction, is one of the best-known Disney tunes of all time.

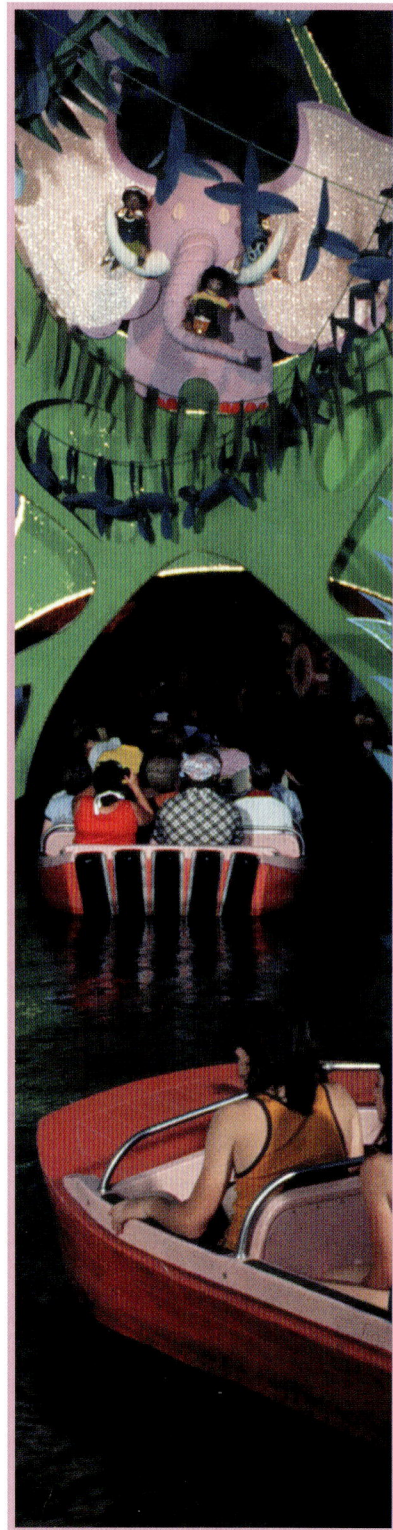

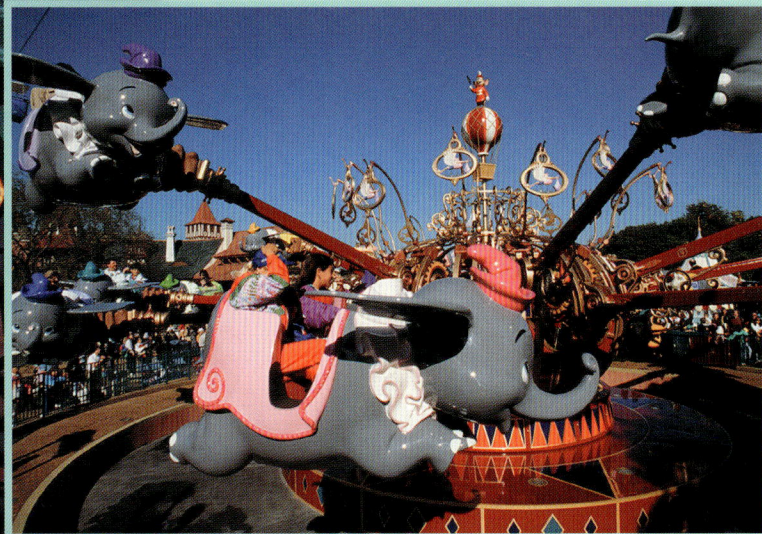

Guests lift off for a spin in Dumbo the Flying Elephant, one of the most popular kiddie attractions in the Magic Kingdom Park. Children love it in large part because they can pilot the giant-eared elephant with the push of a button. Riders hop in oversized teacups, left, for a wild whirl on the Mad Tea Party, inspired by a scene from the classic 1951 film *Alice in Wonderland*.

Mickey's Toontown Fair

Mickey's Toontown Fair is home sweet home to the beloved Disney characters. In this fanciful neighborhood straight out of a Disney animated movie, the county fair is always in town. The colorful Judge's tent is the place to find Mickey, Minnie, and their friends, posing for pictures and signing autographs throughout the day.

Kids of all ages get a chance to cool off on Donald's boat, *Miss Daisy*, named for Donald's sweetheart. The cartoonish boat has enough leaks to squirt most passersby—even the squishy sidewalk is full of surprise fountains. Inside the boat there is a captain's wheel to spin, a map of the Quack Sea, and a steamboat "whistle" that spouts water instead of noise.

H ead to Goofy's Wise Acre Farm for a spin on the *Barnstormer*, a 1920s crop-dusting plane. Fly around a kid-friendly track before bursting through the wall of Goofy's barn—and causing quite a commotion among the chickens.

Tomorrowland ®

Welcome to the "Future That Never Was," inspired by the fantasy world of sci-fi writers and moviemakers of the 1920s and 1930s. Shiny rockets twirl skyward, a soundless train glides by, and guests get the chance to travel back in history or to be catapulted into the cosmos in this exhilarating, space-age land.

The toylike rockets and whirling planets of the Astro Orbiter are timeless favorites of Walt Disney World guests. Riders use the handle to make the open-air rockets rise and lower for a bird's-eye view of the Magic Kingdom. After dark, the soft neon-colored lights of the Astro Orbiter are a distinctive landmark in Tomorrowland.

The ultimate wild ride through the solar system awaits at Space Mountain, rising 180 feet above the Magic Kingdom landscape. Courageous riders twist, turn, and rocket through the inky blackness of a star-filled outer space.

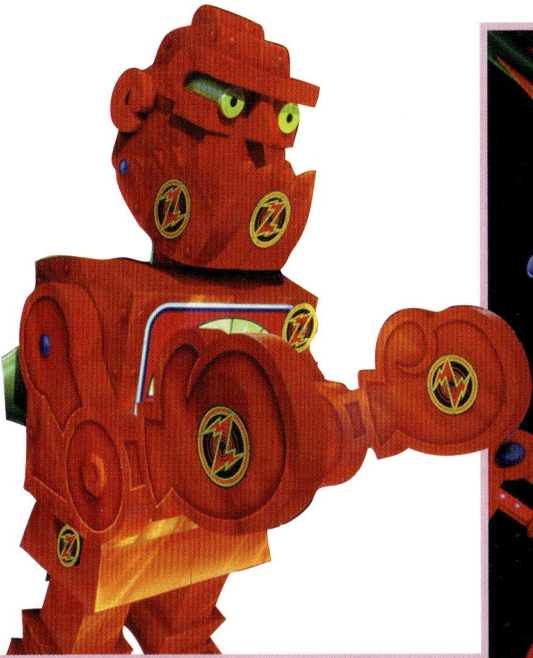

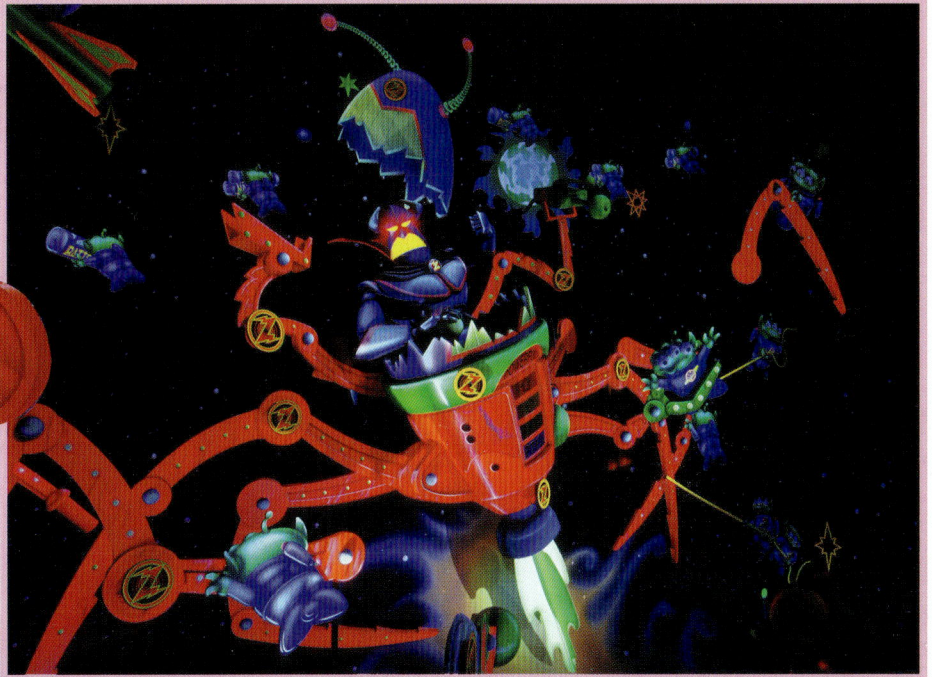

Buzz Lightyear's Space Ranger Spin, above, gives guests a chance to destroy the evil Emperor Zurg in this video game-inspired attraction. Riders fire at targets for points throughout the journey. Below, youngsters get behind the wheel at Tomorrowland Indy Speedway for a dream-come-true lap around the track.

Magic at Night

After the sun goes down, the Vacation Kingdom lights up in dazzling colors and sparkling lights. The twinkling Electrical Water Pageant, opposite left, floats along nightly on Bay Lake, led by King Triton. Below and right, the Fantasy in the Sky Fireworks begin when Tinker Bell flies down from the highest spire of Cinderella Castle to lead off this spectacular nighttime extravaganza. Then, breathtaking fireworks synchronized to classic Disney music explode above Fantasyland in a wonderful world of color.

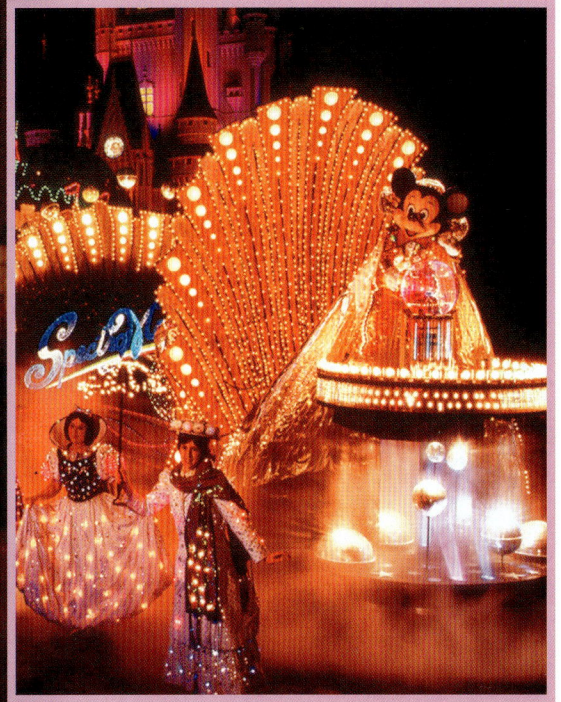

Disney's worlds of wonder and fantasy are vividly illuminated in the SpectroMagic Parade. Mickey Mouse, above, heralds the spectacle, followed by *Aladdin*'s Genie enacting a conductor whose orchestra produces a rainbow of music notes. SpectroMen, left, ride atop glowing whirlyballs, *Fantasia*'s monstrous demon Chernabog spreads his wings to a dramatic 38-foot span, and King Triton and Ariel ride luminescent, sea horse–driven carriages to evade the wicked sea witch Ursula. The brilliant arrays of shimmering fiber-optic and lighting technologies move in concert with a soaring music score.

EPCOT®

• FUTURE WORLD®

There is so much to discover at Epcot®, where Disney fun and imagination are combined with the wonders of the real world. In Future World, cutting-edge technology is tangible, from the hands-on exhibits at Innoventions to a tire-squealing spin on Test Track, the longest, fastest thrill ride in Walt Disney World history.

Take a fascinating tour through the history of communication inside the giant geosphere of Spaceship Earth. Start with the earliest writings of the cavemen, right, view the artistic heights of the Renaissance, above, and journey on through the ages as the ride spirals to the top of the sphere. The finale explores 21st-century communications, a truly amazing system of interactive global networks. Then, riders can step into the Global Neighborhood, left, to try out new technologies.

Touch the technology that's changing the world today in Innoventions, an ever-changing playground. Guests can hop on the Internet, learn how to create a Web page, explore the latest in computers and software, or play the hottest video games.

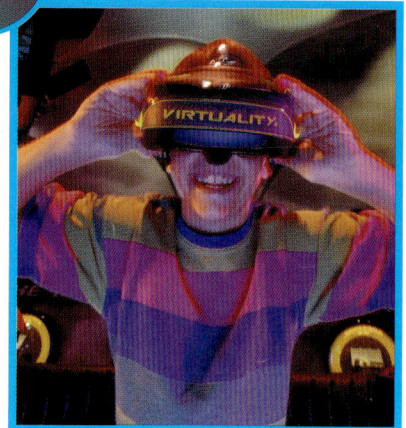

The smells, sights, and sounds of the primeval world come to life in the Universe of Energy, where life-size Audio-Animatronics® dinosaurs are the stars of the show. This fascinating pavilion tells the story of energy, and two acres of solar cells on the roof, left, generate some of the power needed to run the attraction.

TEST TRACK

PRESENTED BY

GM

Buckle up and test a car's limits on the Test Track. Experience everything from an out-of-control skid to a high-speed barrier test. This attraction simulates an automotive proving ground—and you sit in for the dummy rider.

A towering, 72-foot DNA molecule sculpture introduces Wonders of Life, a geodesic dome that is all about living healthfully. Here, two of the top attractions are Cranium Command, starring Buzzy, top, and Body Wars, a flight simulator trip through the human body, above.

The Imagination! pavilion features the hilarious *Honey, I Shrunk the Audience*, where guests experience the feeling of shrinking in this 3-D show full of unforgettable surprises. The pavilion's oddly angled glass pyramids, above, sparkle in the sunlight and create a shining beacon after dark.

Mission: SPACE, presented by HP, allows guests to enjoy the intensity of space travel without ever leaving the planet. In this one-of-a-kind experience, intrepid adventurers assume the roles of captain, engineer, navigator, and pilot, after they begin their simulated voyage with a pulse-racing lift-off. During this "out-of-this-world journey," they encounter challenges faced by real astronauts.

Guests descend to Sea Base Alpha in The Living Seas, where they can look into the world's largest saltwater aquarium—5.7 million gallons. More than 3,000 sea creatures, including dolphins, sharks, angelfish, sea turtles, and rays, entertain spectators.

The Land is the largest pavilion in Future World®, covering six acres. Inside, visitors can take a boat tour through a rain forest and fantastic greenhouses. The whimsical Food Rocks! stage show, bottom left, stars a cast of rock 'n' roll foodies.

CIRCLE OF LIFE
AN ENVIRONMENTAL FABLE

Presented by Nestlé

EPCOT®
WORLD SHOWCASE

Take a whirlwind trip around the globe in World Showcase, where eleven countries celebrate the customs and cuisine of their cultures. Exquisite landscaping and classic architecture transform each pavilion into a picturesque destination, and the variety of entertainment creates a very lively atmosphere on the promenade throughout the day.

Canada

The Hôtel du Canada, left, evokes a feeling of French Canada, and the totem poles, rocky cliffs, running streams, and waterfalls remind guests of the western provinces. A highlight of the pavilion is *O Canada!*, a Circle-Vision 360 film that showcases the rugged beauty of America's neighbor to the north.

United Kingdom

Winding brick streets, quaint buildings, and lovely gardens take visitors back in time. Lively entertainment adds to the ambience. The modern-day U.K. is also well-represented, with a bustling waterfront pub serving a selection of beers and ales and shops stocked with popular wares.

Morocco

The exotic sights and sounds of Africa beckon visitors to this fascinating pavilion. Craftsmen were brought from Morocco to create the intricate mosaics and carved plaster throughout the pavilion, including the imposing re-creation of the Koutoubia Minaret, left, the famous prayer tower in Marrakesh. In the bustling marketplace, woven baskets, hand-knotted rugs, leather sandals, and brass pots are among the many offerings.

France

Turn-of-the-century Paris lends a romantic flair to World Showcase®, recalling the architecture of La Belle Epoque, or "beautiful era", in the last decades of the 19th century. The scent of freshly baked croissants and pastries draws guests to the wonderful Patisserie, where there is outdoor seating. Nearby, a movie theater offers an enchanting journey across France.

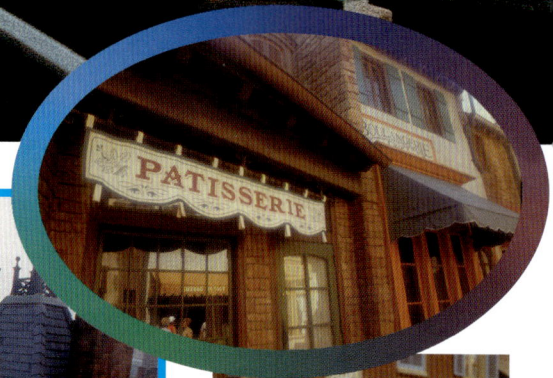

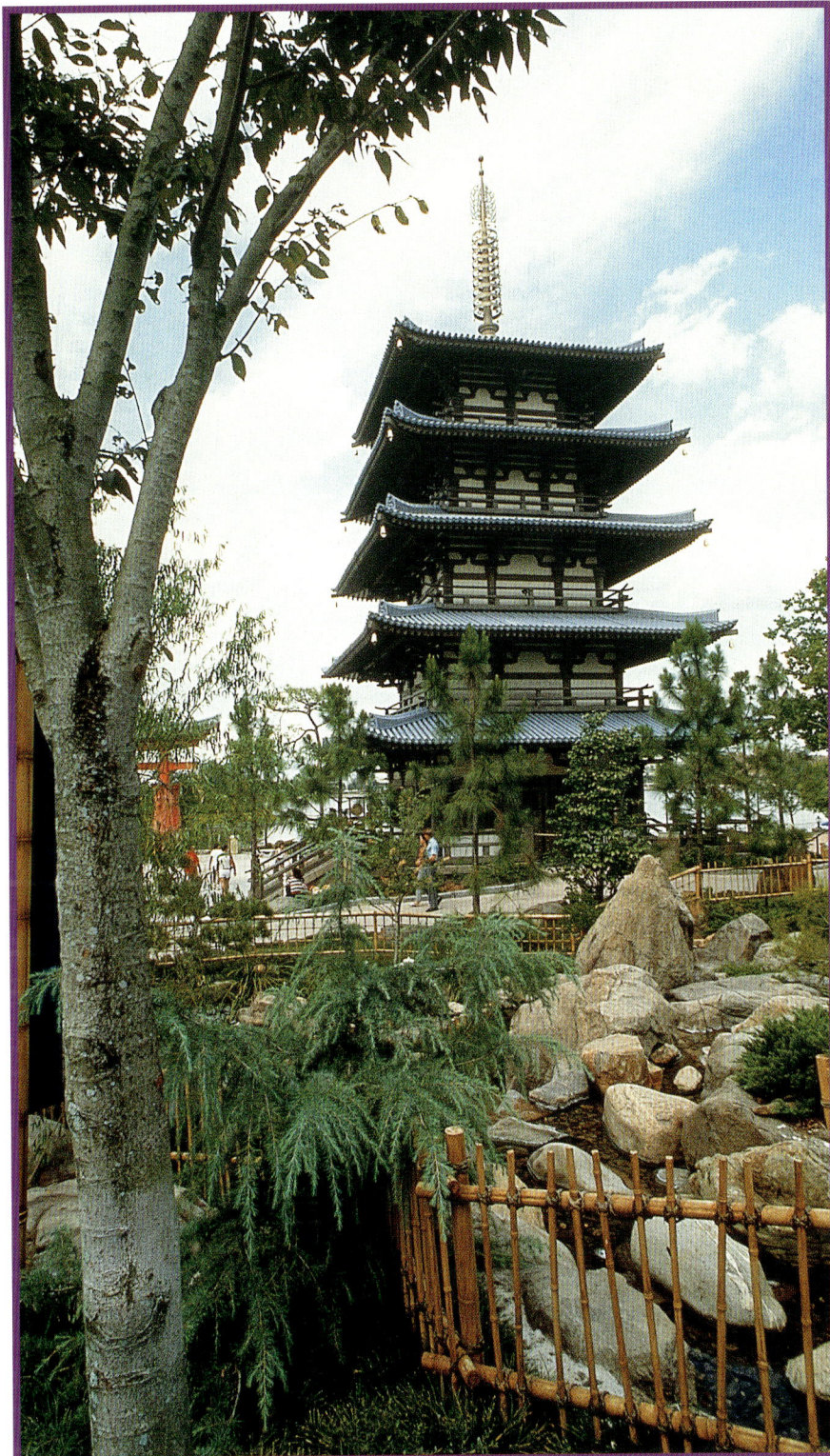

Japan

A brilliant blue-winged pagoda, left, leads guests to Japan. After a stroll through pathways in the peaceful Japanese gardens, guests can shop in the spacious Mitsukoshi department store, a direct offshoot of the three-centuries-old retail firm. The torii gate near World Showcase Lagoon is modeled after the Itsukushima Shrine in Hiroshima Bay.

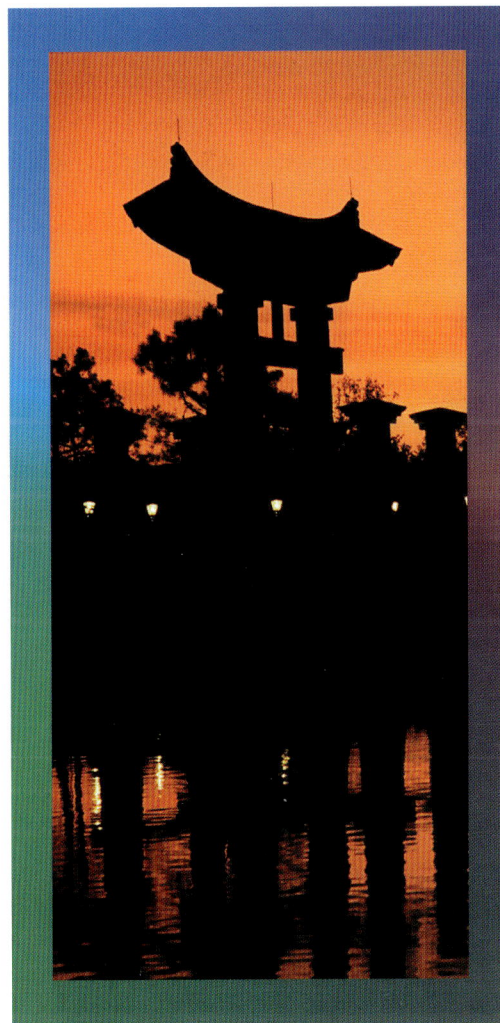

The American Adventure

The centerpiece of World Showcase®, The American Adventure celebrates the American spirit in one of Disney's most sophisticated shows. Benjamin Franklin and Mark Twain are the lifelike Audio-Animatronics® narrators, nostalgically recalling great moments in U.S. history.

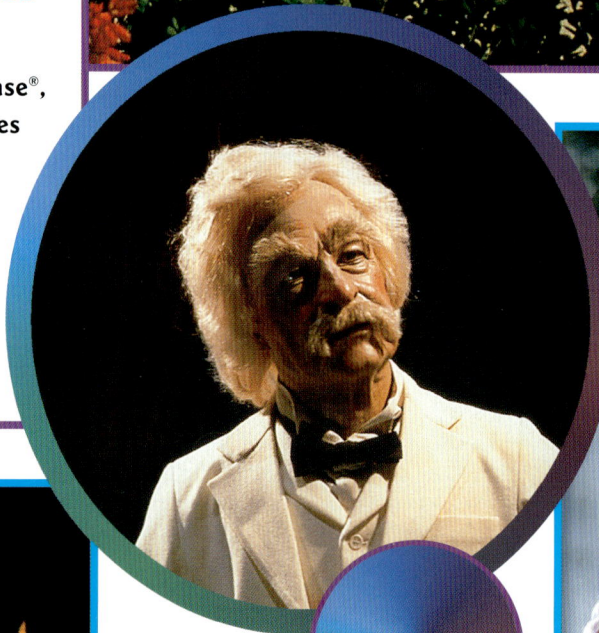

Italy

Moorings that look like barber poles and Venetian gondolas set the stage in Italy, where a stroll across the wide piazza is like a quick course in Italian architecture. Inspired by St. Mark's Square in Venice, this splendid pavilion includes a replica of the 1309 Doge's Palace. A smaller version of the Campanile is topped by a delicate sculpted angel covered in real gold leaf, which shines in the sunlight. Even the fountain statue of the sea god Neptune is a re-creation of the original.

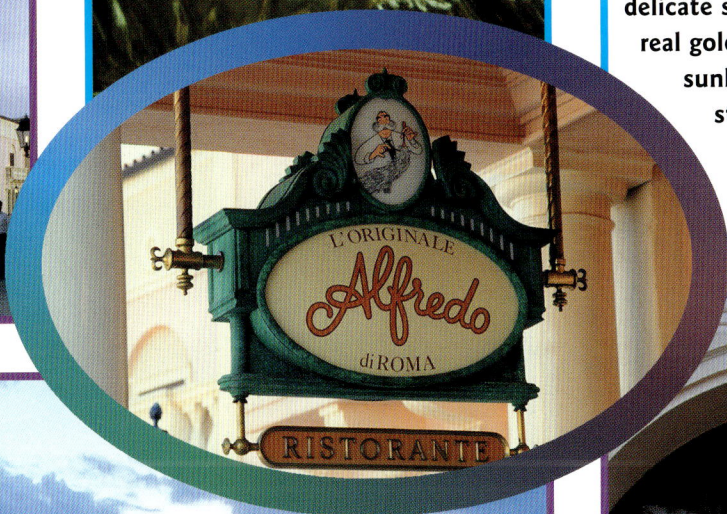

Germany

This picturesque pavilion is like a charming fairy tale village. Gingerbread-decorated shops, a glockenspiel that chimes on the hour, and a biergarten—much like those found at Munich's famed Oktoberfest—enliven the atmosphere. The statue in the middle of the town square, right, honors St. George, the patron saint of soldiers.

China

More than 6,000 years of cultural heritage are showcased in the ancient land of China. Guests are drawn to the graceful Hall of Prayers for Good Harvests, inspired by the opulent Temple of Heaven in Beijing. Tranquil gardens, traditional entertainment, and an awe-inspiring film await discovery.

Norway

Experience the rugged beauty of the Land of the Midnight Sun. Reminiscent of the towns of Oslo and Bergen, this pavilion includes a castle inspired by Oslo's famed 14th-century Akershus. Inside, you can board a dragon-headed longboat for a fun journey through Norway's history and folklore.

Mexico

Lush landscaping and spectacular pre-Columbian pyramids pave the way to the pavilion's charming interior. It is perpetually twilight in the lively plaza, and visitors are often serenaded by a mariachi band. From a candlelit riverside dining room, guests watch boats float by in El Río del Tiempo, an attraction that celebrates Mexican life.

The nighttime sky ignites when IllumiNations: Reflections of Earth celebrates the glory of our world in a spectacular extravaganza of fire and light. This one-of-a-kind entertainment presents the entire history of our planet from its creation to the present and looks toward the future, with a dazzling mix of special effects, colorful lasers, brilliant fireworks, water fountains, and fiery torches, all choreographed to a stirring original musical score.

Disney-MGM Studios®

Experience the glitz, glamour, and excitement of show business at Disney-MGM Studios. Stroll down Hollywood Boulevard, watch as classic Disney characters are brought to life through the magic of animation, or plummet 13 stories down the elevator shaft of The Hollywood Tower Hotel.

The Great Movie Ride is one of Disney's most elaborate ride-through attractions, showcasing some of Hollywood's most memorable movie moments. The dazzling blue Sorcerer Hat, opposite, that caps the end of Hollywood Boulevard stands 122 feet tall. The newest park icon represents the entertainment wizardry of Disney, which is captured throughout the shows and attractions at the park.

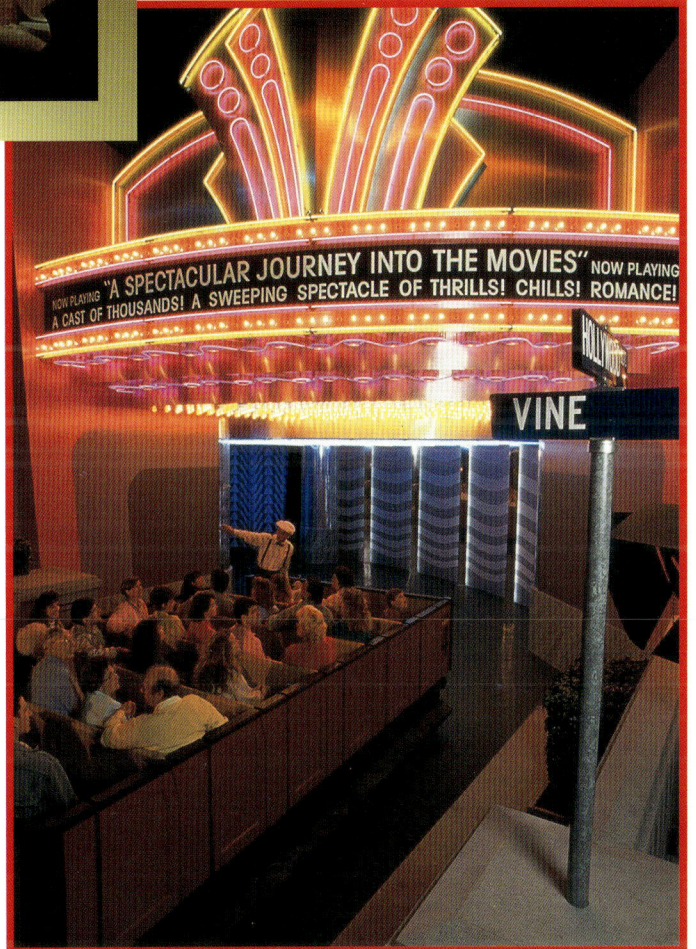

Guests get an insider's view of real-life filmmaking, left, as they view animators at work on the next generation of Disney animated films in The Magic of Disney Animation. The Disney-MGM Studios Backlot Tour, below center, travels through a behind-the-scenes look at movie and television production, including the action-packed Catastrophe Canyon. Tram riders learn firsthand how natural disasters are created at the studios when they're stranded during the filming of a flash flood and some 70,000 gallons of water are unleashed.

THE MAGIC OF

Disney

ANIMATION

Live stage shows bring Disney's classic animated films to life. Voyage of the Little Mermaid, left, pits Ursula the sea witch against the mermaid Ariel. Beauty and the Beast—Live on Stage, below right, tells the story of Belle and the Beast in a romantic, high-spirited musical.

Jim Henson's Muppet*Vision 3D TM & © 2001 The Jim Henson Company

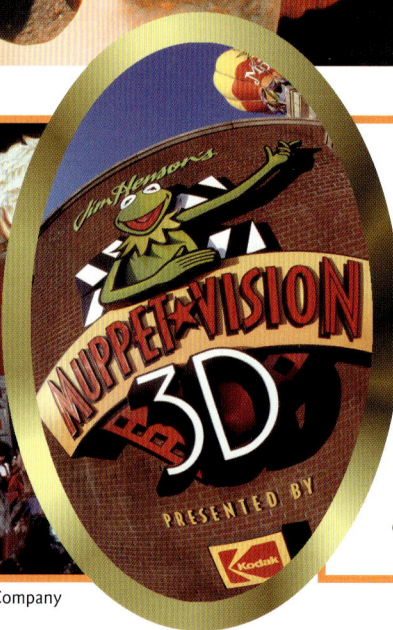

Youngsters can get lost in the colossal backyard of Honey, I Shrunk the Kids Movie Set Adventure, a play area where blades of grass are 20 feet high. Left, Jim Henson's Muppet*Vision 3D combines puppets, advanced 3-D action, and in-theater special effects to showcase the wild antics of Henson's legendary characters.

Pros show off thrilling stunts in the Indiana Jones™ Epic Stunt Spectacular! The death-defying heroics of classic adventure films are demonstrated on the gigantic movie set of this action-packed live production. At right, Indiana Jones keeps the audience on the edge of their seats as he dodges a 12 foot tall rolling ball. Below, a truck gets blown up as Indy and his sweetheart escape in the explosive finale.

Passengers buckle up for a wild galactic journey to the Moon of Endor in Star Tours, below. The attraction combines flight simulator technology and a thrill-a-second motion picture to create an uproarious flight into deep space. Props inspired by *Star Wars* movies set the stage, right, as visitors enter the attraction.

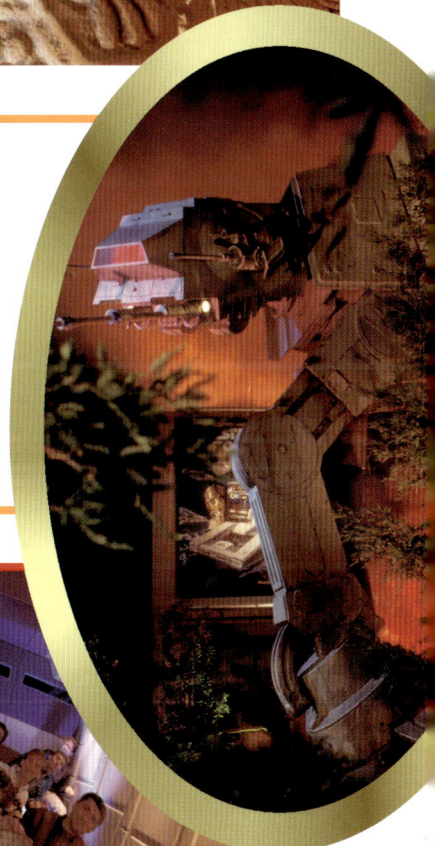

Who Wants To Be A Millionaire - Play It! begins when the guest with the fastest finger is chosen from the audience to land in the "hot seat" and play for prizes as the popular game show is re-created in all its suspenseful spectacle. Players still have three lifelines for help, but when they "phone a friend," the call will go to a complete stranger who happens to be passing by outside the theater!

Fantasmic!, a nighttime water spectacle featuring Mickey Mouse in a tale of fantasy and fright, comes to life in the Hollywood Hills amphitheater. The nightly extravaganza explores Mickey's imagination from the whimsical ways of his colorful friends to the darkness of Disney villains.

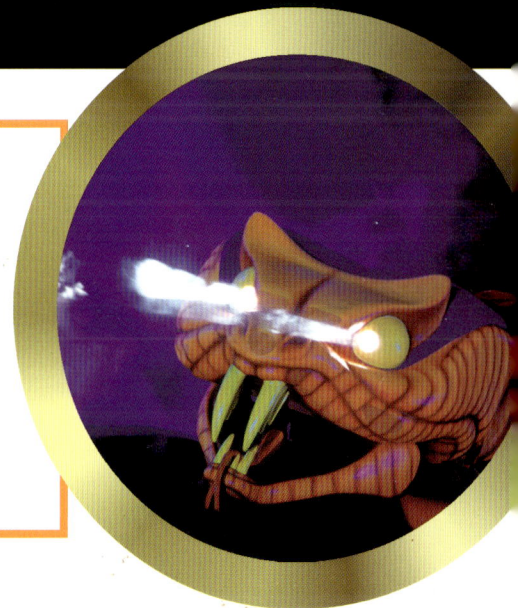

Climb the charts on the Rock 'n' Roller Coaster® Starring Aerosmith. This wild experience features a high-speed launch and multiple complete inversions, sending riders twirling into the Hollywood night. The indoor roller coaster twists, turns, and tumbles upside-down to the driving beat of an original rock soundtrack written just for this attraction by Aerosmith.

The Twilight Zone Tower of Terror

A 13-story plunge awaits guests brave enough to venture into the Hollywood Tower Hotel at the end of Sunset Boulevard. Great special effects throughout are reminiscent of the television series, but all pales in comparison to the terrifying drops—not once, not twice, but sometimes three times down an elevator shaft.

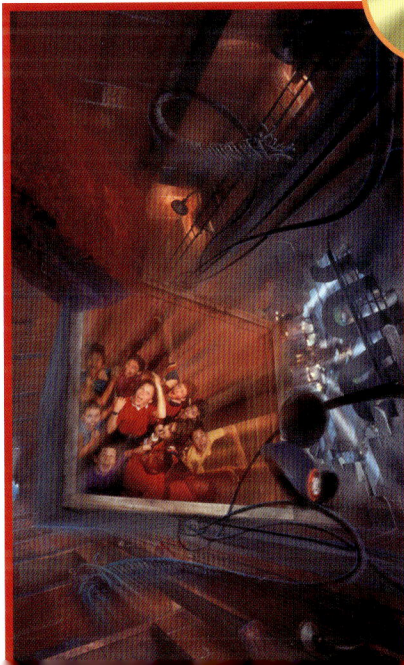

The Twilight Zone® is a registered trademark of CBS, Inc. and is used pursuant to a license from CBS, Inc.

DISNEY'S ANIMAL KINGDOM® THEME PARK

Lace up your walking shoes and prepare to explore five exciting lands of adventure in Disney's Animal Kingdom Theme Park. The intriguing worlds of wild and fanciful creatures come to life on thrill rides and on an authentic African safari, in theaters brimming with colorful entertainment, and through up-close encounters with the animal stars of Disney feature animation classics. Wonder and whimsy reign in this fourth and newest major theme park.

The park's fun-filled lands radiate from the centrally located Discovery Island™ area. In the center, towering 145 feet above guests, is the Tree of Life park icon. Carved with a swirling tapestry of more than 300 animal forms, it represents the awe-inspiring tale of all the earth's animals and the interconnectedness of all living things. Brightly colored shops and restaurants are adorned with thousands of hand-painted wooden folk art carvings—a fusion of pre-Columbian, Peruvian, African, and Polynesian forms—crafted on the island of Bali by native craftsmen.

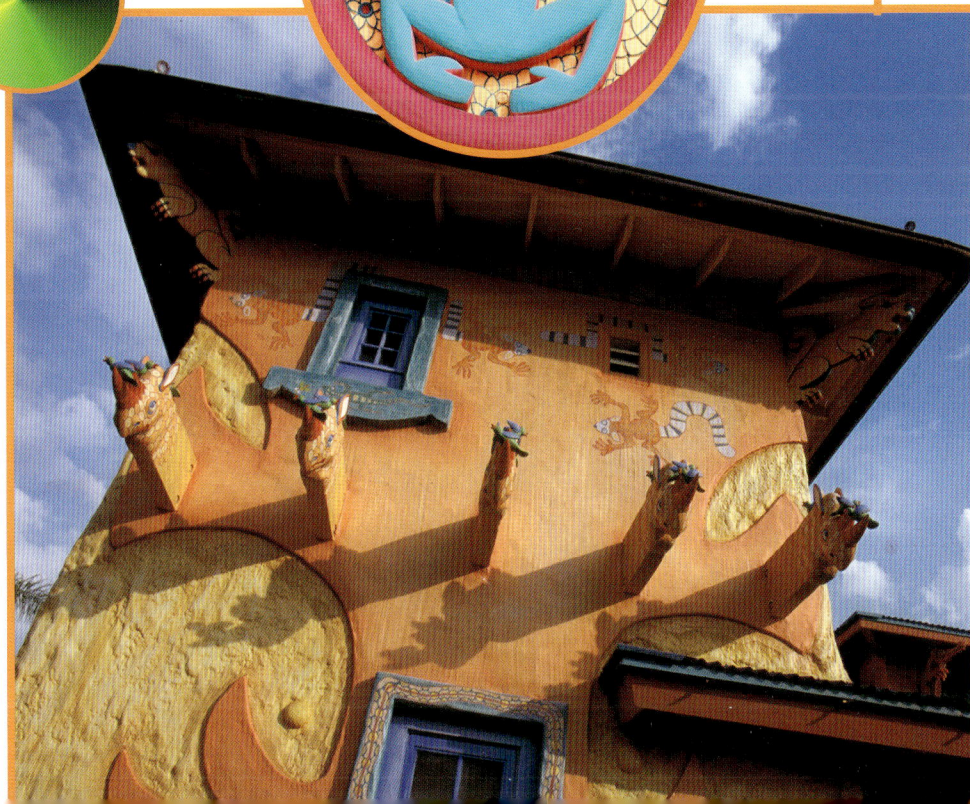

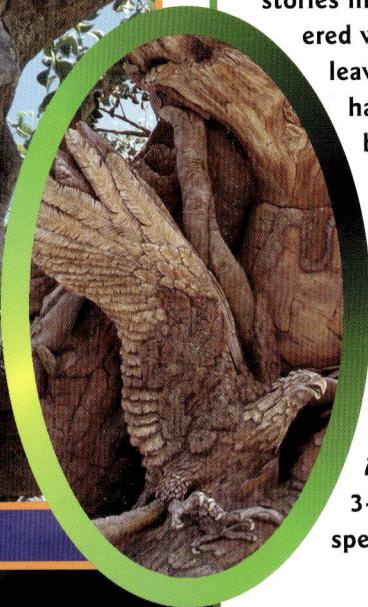

The graceful Tree of Life rises 14 stories into the sky, and is covered with more than 100,000 leaves, all attached by hand to more than 8,000 branches. Twenty artists created the intricate carvings. Inside the tree is a hilarious special effects experience, *It's Tough to be a Bug!*®, that spins an amusing yarn using Audio-Animatronics®, 3-D film, and in-theater special effects.

Take a leisurely stroll through the lush vegetation of the Tree of Life Garden where Red kangaroos, capybaras, Galapagos Tortoises, and lemurs flourish, and frolicking otters can be observed aboveground as well as through an underwater viewing area. The striking pink of a flock of flamingos, left, provides a dramatic contrast to the rich greens and browns of the Tree of Life.

Camp Minnie-Mickey, a child's paradise of woodland trails, is the place to meet favorite characters. It is also home to the enormously popular Festival of the Lion King (based on the classic Disney film), a Broadway-style musical filled with energetic singers, dancers, and acrobatic performers, many costumed in colorful African tribal garb.

WELCOME TO
HARAMBE
PORT OF EAST AFRICA

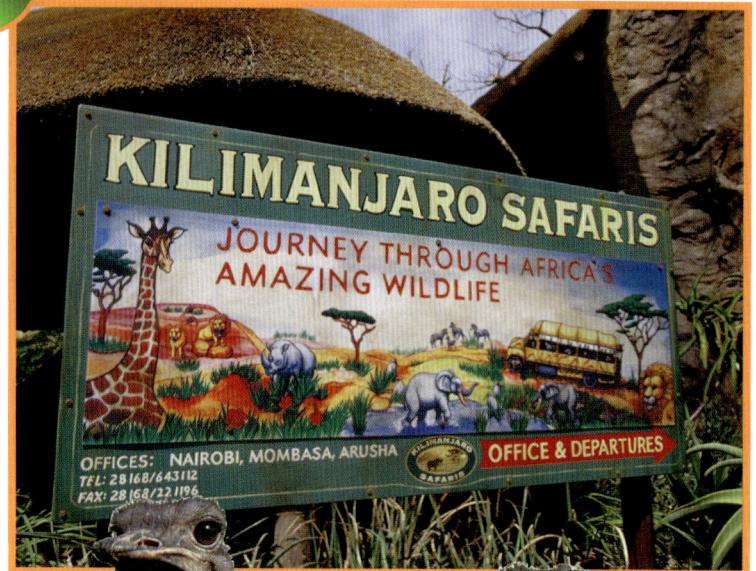

KILIMANJARO SAFARIS
JOURNEY THROUGH AFRICA'S
AMAZING WILDLIFE

OFFICES: NAIROBI, MOMBASA, ARUSHA
TEL: 28168/643112
FAX: 28 168/22 1196

OFFICE & DEPARTURES

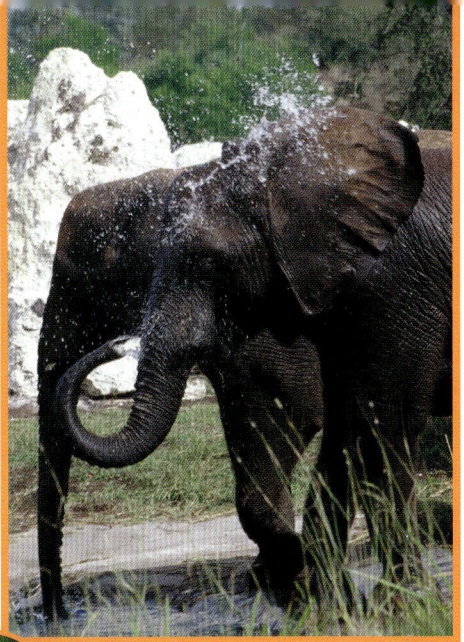

Kilimanjaro Safaris® is where guests really get to see the hundreds of animals that are living under trees, wallowing in waterholes, and grazing the soft savanna grasses. The adventure begins in Harambe Village, then it's off down a dirt trail in an open-sided truck to explore 110 acres of African forest. The exciting show culminates in a race to save an elephant herd from a gang of dangerous ivory poachers.

Pangani Forest Exploration Trail® leads guests through a very lush bamboo jungle inhabited by two troops of lowland gorillas, foraging through the trees just inches away. The winding trail also offers an intimate look at rare birds, mammals, fish, and reptiles, many too small or too shy to be seen on the safari ride.

The Wildlife Express® steam train, right, takes visitors to Rafiki's Planet Watch for an up-close look at how the park's animals are kept happy and healthy. There are several interactive areas, including the Affection Section, left, where guests can meet and pet small domestic animals.

Gibbons, above, emit deep-throated hoots as they swing from a Nepalese-styled monument tower to the ruins of a Thai-inspired temple in the mythical village of Anandapur in Asia. Another inhabitant is the Komodo dragon, below, which can grow up to 12 feet long and is the largest lizard in the world.

Revered tigers roam near the crumbling walls of a palace on the Maharajah Jungle Trek, a breathtaking journey through the lush home of myriad animal and bird species. In this superb rain forest environment, Indonesia, Thailand, Nepal, and India are all represented through architecture, ruins, and animal carvings.

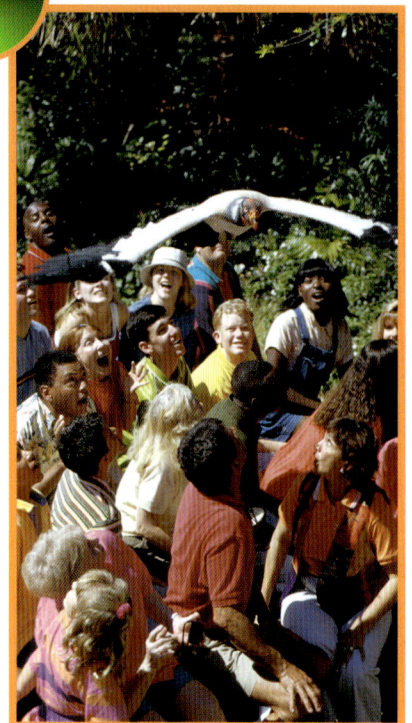

An aviary can be found within the Maharajah Jungle Trek, top, giving guests an up-close and personal experience with some feathered friends from Asia. The Flights of Wonder show, above, highlights the beauty and diversity of birds. The setting is a crumbling Asian fort, where macaws, ibis, and other birds emerge from alcoves to soar high overhead. Although the show is carefully rehearsed, the birds are taught to show off their natural talent, not to do tricks.

Giant rafts launch guests into the turbulent Chakranadi River for a wild, wet ride through a jungle habitat on the Kali River Rapids® Attraction in Asia. Rafters get a fun—and wet—ride, with surprises around every turn as the raft twists and spins through the river, narrowly avoiding disaster in a burning forest.

Welcome to DinoLand U.S.A.®, a lively celebration of our fascination with dinosaurs. Far left, 50-foot-tall brachiosaurus bones straddle the entrance to this land. Kids can literally dig into the past at The Boneyard® Dig Site, opposite top, an open-air playground where there are replicas of fossils and reconstructed skeletons, or buy dinosaur toys, trinkets, and T-shirts at Chester & Hester's, above left. Those wacky dino-maniacs also bring you Dino-Rama!, right, a cretaceously crazy fun fair complete with midway games and rides. Take a wacky time warp to a prehysterical era on the Primeval Whirl, near left, or see a dino "soar" on the TriceraTop Spin, above right.

Trademark TARZAN Owned by Edgar Rice Burroughs, Inc.; Used by Permission.

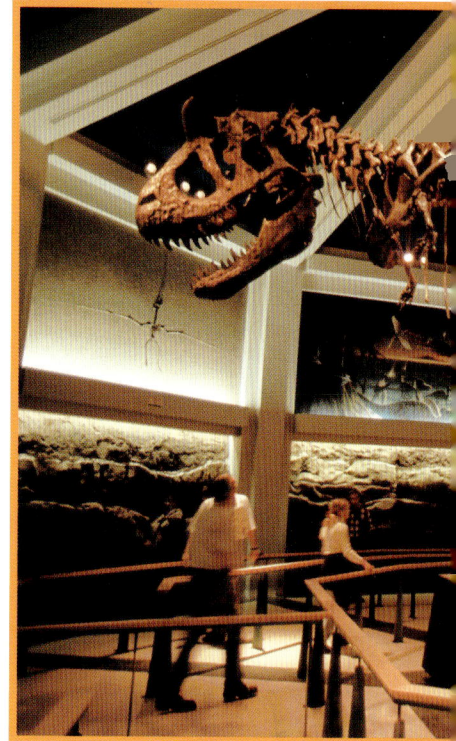

Tarzan™ Rocks! brings the emotion of the hit animated film *Tarzan*™ to life in a high-energy and high-flying extravaganza performed in Theater in the Wild®. Singers, dancers, gymnasts, aerialists, and in-line skaters join Tarzan™, Jane, and Terk on stage, as action spills into and above the audience. The four-act show features five songs from the film's sound-track, including the hit single "*You'll Be in My Heart*."

Buckle up for a breath-taking, high-speed adventure in Dinosaur, a wild journey back in time. Guests enter the Dino Institute's rotunda, left, which depicts the extinction of the dinosaurs, and then board a Time Rover. The adventure goes awry when a hail of meteors strikes this vehicle, which careens off course and plunges recklessly downhill into a dark jungle. A monstrous carnotaurus pursues the Time Rover, giving it just seconds to make it safely back through time.

The Rest of the World

Drift over a tropical reef, take a fantasy spin on a race-car speedway track, or escape on a fabulous cruise . . . magical adventures await beyond the four Walt Disney World theme parks. Whether you are looking for more ways to have fun or a little peace and quiet, the Vacation Kingdom represents the most complete resort destination in the world.

Plunge into fun on the Summit Plummet water slide, opposite page, the Toboggan Racers, above left, or the double-humped Slush Gusher, above right, at Disney's Blizzard Beach® Water Park. Disney's Typhoon Lagoon® Water Park, center, hosts a "wateropolis" of thrilling attractions, beneath the shadow of Mt. Mayday. Guests come face-to-face with all the colorful creatures of the Caribbean when they snorkel in Shark Reef, left.

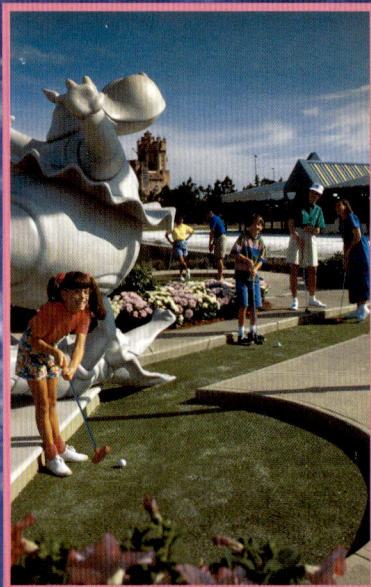

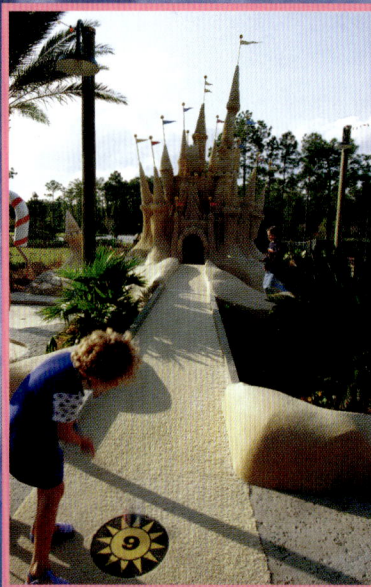

Sorcerer Mickey and other characters from the animated classic film *Fantasia* adorn two 18-hole miniature golf courses in the whimsical Fantasia Gardens Miniature Golf Course. Newcomers and veterans alike find surprises around every sculpted corner. Near Disney's Blizzard Beach Water Park is Disney's Winter Summerland, two 18-hole golf courses—one with a zany, snow-clad theme, the other with a more tropical, holiday theme, complete with festive ornaments hanging from palm trees.

Variety is the name of the game at Disney's Wide World of Sports™ Complex, the ultimate destination for competitors and fans alike. The 200-acre facility can host more than 30 sports, from archery to wrestling. Guests can participate in the Richard Petty Driving Experience at the Walt Disney World Speedway.

The magic continues 24 hours a day at the Walt Disney World themed resorts. The Spanish-style villas at Disney's Coronado Springs Resort, top left, serve up a spicy southwestern atmosphere. The festive decorations of Disney's Port Orleans Resort–Riverside, right, evoke the playful fun of Mardi Gras while the charm of historic New Orleans is portrayed at its neighbor, Disney's Port Orleans Resort–French Quarter. Disney's All-Star Movies Resort includes giant icons from favorite Disney films such as Pongo from *101 Dalmatians*, top right.

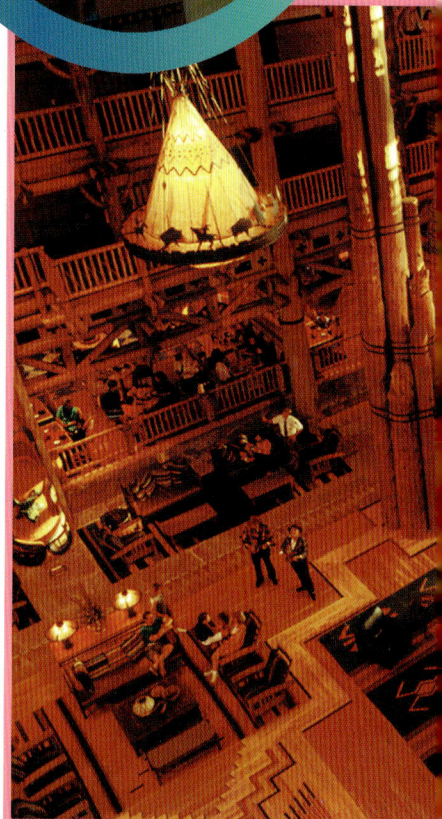

Hayrides, horseback riding, and a petting farm are among the fun-filled activities to enjoy at Disney's Fort Wilderness Resort and Campground, top left. Disney's Old Key West Resort, bottom right, retains the cozy, laid-back ambience of Florida's seaside villages while the rustic lobby of Disney's Wilderness Lodge transports visitors to the Pacific Northwest, bottom left. The exotic details of Disney's Polynesian Resort, inset, establish its balmy tropical mood.

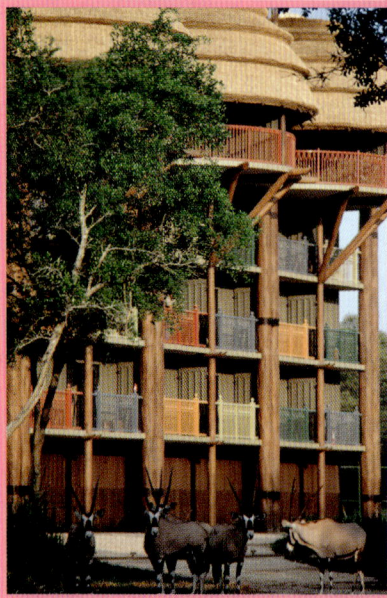

Disney's BoardWalk Inn and Villas Resort, above, captures the character of a 1930s Mid-Atlantic coastal resort where the award-winning The Flying Fish Cafe, bottom right, is the place to dine. Disney's Yacht and Beach Club Resorts, right, and Disney's Grand Floridian Resort & Spa, opposite page top left, offer distinctive architecture and relaxing amenities. Disney's Animal Kingdom Lodge, left and below, provides a personal platform from numerous rooms for viewing animals and nature.

Disney's Contemporary Resort, top right, in the Magic Kingdom resort area, offers guests a spectacular view of Cinderella Castle. Located on 200 lushly landscaped acres, the five brightly colored "villages" of Disney's Caribbean Beach Resort, middle, surround the beautiful Barefoot Bay Lake. The name of the game is athletics at Disney's All-Star Sports Resort, bottom right, where the guest rooms feature sports-themed bedspreads, megaphone light fixtures, and artwork depicting sports scenes.

High-energy Downtown Disney® West Side, above, is a truly outstanding mix of entertainment, world-class restaurants, nightclubs, and great shopping adventures. DisneyQuest® Indoor Interactive Theme Park, promising a whole new kind of virtual fun, is one of the most popular spots. Guests begin their journey at the Ventureport, right, which leads to five floors of amazing entertainment technology.